THE UNDERGROUND RAILROAD AND SLAVERY THROUGH PRIMARY SOURCES

Carin T. Ford

Enslow Publishers, Inc.
40 Industrial Road
Box 398
Berkeley Heights, NJ 07922
USA

http://www.enslow.com

Original edition published as *Slavery and the Underground Railroad: Bound for Freedom* in 2004.

Library of Congress Cataloging-in-Publication Data

Ford, Carin T.
 The Underground Railroad and slavery through primary sources / Carin T. Ford.
   p. cm. — (The Civil War through primary sources)
 Includes bibliographical references and index.
 Summary: "Examines slavery and the Underground Railroad in the United States, including slavery in early America, the difficult daily life of a slave, the creation of the Underground Railroad, and the courageous people who helped slaves escape to freedom"—Provided by publisher.
  ISBN 978-0-7660-4127-1
 1. Underground Railroad—Juvenile literature. 2. Fugitive slaves—United States—Juvenile literature. 3. Slavery—United States—History—Juvenile literature. I. Title.
 E450.F695 2013
 973.7'115—dc23

                    2012036349

Future editions:
Paperback ISBN: 978-1-4644-0185-5
EPUB ISBN: 978-1-4645-1098-4
Single-User PDF ISBN: 978-1-4646-1098-1
Multi-User PDF ISBN: 978-0-7660-5727-2

Printed in China

122012 Leo Paper Group, Heshan City, Guangdong, China

10 9 8 7 6 5 4 3 2 1

To Our Readers: We have done our best to make sure all Internet Addresses in this book were active and appropriate when we went to press. However, the author and the publisher have no control over and assume no liability for the material available on those Internet sites or on other Web sites they may link to. Any comments or suggestions can be sent by email to comments@enslow.com or to the address on the back cover.

Illustration Credits: Enslow Publishers, Inc., p. 29; The Granger Collection, NYC, pp. 22, 30; Library of Congress Prints and Photographs, pp. 1, 2–3, 4, 5, 7, 10, 12, 15, 19, 23, 24, 26, 32, 34, 36, 38; Library of Congress Rare Books and Manuscripts Division, p. 27; Manuscripts and Archives Division, New York Public Library, Astor, Lenox and Tilden Foundations, p. 16; *Narrative of the Life of Frederick Douglass, An American Slave*, © 1845, frontispiece, p. 20; National Archives and Records Administration, pp. 13, 40.

Cover Illustration: The Granger Collection, NYC (Painting of slaves traveling on the Underground Railroad).

CONTENTS

LOOK FOR THIS SYMBOL **PRIMARY SOURCE** **TO FIND THE PRIMARY SOURCES THROUGHOUT THIS BOOK.**

In this May 1862 photo, Confederate general Thomas F. Drayton (front left in uniform) stands with his slaves at a plantation in Hilton Head, South Carolina. When the Civil War began in 1861, slavery had existed in the United States for nearly 250 years.

CHAPTER 1

THE GROWTH OF SLAVERY

There was so much to be done in the American colonies—cities to be built, farmland to be cleared and planted. Who would do it? Many people came from Europe as indentured servants. This means they promised to work for several years in exchange for food and housing. After that time, they would be free. Other people were brought to the colonies in chains. They were forced to work for no pay. They would never earn their freedom. They were slaves.

A boat carrying twenty African slaves landed on the shores of Jamestown, Virginia, in August 1619. One hundred slaves had begun the journey, but eighty of them died along the way.

The voyage across the Atlantic Ocean was terrible. Men, women, and children were packed together below the ship's deck. They had little food or water. There was hardly any air to breathe. Sickness spread quickly from one person to another. Of the 15 million African people who were sold into slavery, nearly 4 million died while sailing across the ocean.[1]

The twenty slaves who stepped off the boat in Virginia were the first Africans to arrive in the American colonies. The Dutch trader who had brought them exchanged the slaves for food.[2]

For the next sixty years, only a small number of Africans were brought to America. Indentured servants did most of the work in the colonies. But after a while, landowners felt they could get more for their money by buying slaves.[3]

Most African slaves worked on farms in the American colonies. Especially in the South, crops such as tobacco and rice grew well.

The conditions aboard slave ships were inhumane. Slaves were packed belowdecks with virtually no food or water, sweltering temperatures, unsanitary conditions, and little air to breathe in the complete darkness. This drawing shows the crowded space where slaves were forcibly kept on a British slave ship in 1788.

On Board a Slave Ship

Millions of African people died on the trip from Africa to the Americas. Chained together below deck, the slaves were packed in so tightly that they had no room to move. On one ship, the captives were given only a teacup of water every three days. With the temperature often climbing to 120°F on these voyages, most slaves died from lack of water. Often, there was so little air that candles would not burn and the people could hardly breathe. So many dead bodies were tossed overboard each day that sharks followed the slave ships across the Atlantic Ocean.

Large numbers of workers were needed in the fields to do the planting, plowing, hoeing, and harvesting of the crops.

African slaves were cheap in the 1600s, and there seemed to be an endless supply of them. So the slave trade grew. The traders made a good profit. They could buy a slave in Africa for about $25, then sell that slave in the colonies for $150. By 1800, slaves were selling for $500. Fifty years later, the price jumped to $800.[4] As the years passed, close to half a million slaves would end up in the United States.

The slave trade worked well for the traders and the colonists, but it was horrible for the African people. They were bought and sold on the auction block like animals. They were beaten, whipped, and half-starved. Any child born to a slave mother became a slave, too. Families were torn apart. Children were sold away from their parents.

Over time, laws were passed in the colonies making it impossible for any Africans—even those who had come to America as indentured servants—to earn their freedom. They would be property for the rest of their lives.

Colonial Slavery

★ By 1750, slavery was legal in all thirteen of the American colonies.

★ No legal record has ever been found stating that a white man or woman in America had to spend his or her life as a slave.[5]

★ In the U.S. Constitution, each slave counted for only three-fifths of a person.

By the mid-1700s, about one of every five Americans was a slave.[6] Most slaves lived in the South, where they labored on farms and large plantations. Not as many slaves were needed to work in the homes and businesses of the North.

Still, it seemed as if slavery was on its way out. The American Revolution had filled people's heads with thoughts of freedom and justice. A growing number of people wanted to end slavery. By the 1780s, most Northern states had already done away with it. Also, the fields in the South had been planted so often that the soil was worn out. Farmers could not grow as much, so fewer workers were needed.

Then, in 1793, Eli Whitney invented the cotton gin. This was a machine that removed the seeds from the cotton. With a machine—instead of a person—doing the work, fifty times more cotton could be cleaned every day. Southern farmers could now make a lot of money selling cotton.

Many farmers switched to growing cotton almost overnight. Even if their fields were worn out, they planted rows and rows of cotton. As the cotton industry grew, so did the need for slaves. They no longer picked the seeds from the cotton, but hundreds of

In this 1862 photo, African-American slaves work in a pile of cotton, preparing it for the cotton gin at Smith's plantation in Port Royal Island, South Carolina.

Abolition

★ Abolish means to end something or get rid of it. People who wanted to put an end to slavery were called abolitionists.

★ Even in colonial days, some people spoke out against slavery. Later, in the 1800s, many people became abolitionists.

slaves were still needed to work on the many cotton plantations in the South.

By 1860, the South was turning out 4 million bales of cotton every year. This was almost two-thirds of all the cotton grown in the world. It was no wonder the South was called "King Cotton."

At the time the cotton gin was invented, in 1793, there were 400,000 slaves in the United States. By the time the Civil War broke out, in 1861, there were 4 million slaves. One out of every three people living in the South was a slave.[7]

CHAPTER 2

THE LIFE OF A SLAVE

Not all slaves were treated the same. House servants were given better food and clothing than the other slaves. Their job was to clean, cook, wait on their masters, and care for the masters' children.

Craftsmen came next in importance. These were skilled workers such as blacksmiths, carpenters, shoemakers, weavers, butchers, gunsmiths, potters, and painters.

Most slaves worked in the fields. They were treated the worst. Field hands spent their days planting, plowing, and picking crops.

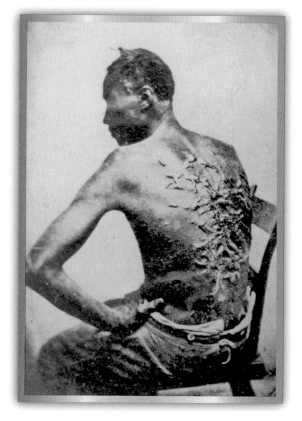

Slaves, especially field workers, often received brutal punishments. Overseers carried whips or other weapons. In this photo, a runaway slave from Mississippi, Gordon (no last name given), shows the scars from beatings he received as a slave.

They were watched by men called overseers, who carried whips, and often guns and knives.

Field workers needed to be out in the fields as soon as there was enough light to see. Anyone showing up late was likely to get whipped. Even if slaves felt tired or sick, they could not stop to rest. When there was a full moon, they often worked until the middle of the night.[1]

William Wells Brown was a house slave who worked for several slave masters in Kentucky. His mother worked in the fields. One day, his mother was punished for getting to work just ten minutes late. "Though the field was some distance from the house, I could

Fugitive Slave Laws

Laws were passed to help return fugitive, or runaway, slaves:

1793 LAW: An owner only had to show proof that a slave was his property. Many Northern states did not like this law. They made their own laws instead, and the South was angry.

1850 LAW: Stricter punishments made more Northerners obey. Anyone caught helping a runaway slave had to pay a large sum of money or go to jail.

hear every crack of the whip, and every groan and cry of my poor mother," he said.[2]

Not all slaves were beaten. Some were treated kindly. However, many slaves lived with cruel masters. Often, masters branded their slaves. This means they labeled their slaves by burning a mark into their skin. If the slave ran away and was captured, the brand showed who the owner was.

For most farmers, punishing slaves was just a regular part of the day. William Byrd, a Virginia planter, wrote in his diary: "3 September 1709. I read some geometry . . . I ate roast chicken for dinner. In the afternoon I beat Jenny for throwing water on the couch."[3]

Life was very grim for slaves. It was against the law for a slave to learn how to read or write. They were not allowed to have books, pens, paper, or ink. Masters were afraid that if slaves could read and write, they would spread news and messages to other slaves. They might plan to fight against their masters or run away.

Most slaves lived in wooden shacks with dirt floors. There were no beds—just a pile of straw and old rags thrown into the corner. Clothing was handed out twice a year. Each man wore

Five generations of slaves pose for a photo outside a shack in Beaufort, South Carolina. Houses for slaves were often wooden shacks with dirt floors.

Please to let Benjamin McDaniel pass to Dr. Henkal's in New-Market, Shenandoah County, Va. and return on Monday. or Tuesday ninth to Montpellier, for Mrs. Madison.

June 1st 1843.

This slave pass was given to Benjamin McDaniel to travel from Montpellier to New Market, Shenandoah County, Virginia, on June 1, 1843. Slaves caught leaving a plantation without a pass could be thrown into jail or shot.

The Slave Codes

Laws known as Slave Codes were passed in the South to keep slaves from rebelling or running away. Slaves needed a written pass whenever they left the plantation. If they were caught without one, they could be thrown into jail or shot. If a slave ran away or attacked a white person, he could be whipped or branded. Also, slave owners were allowed to interrupt any gathering of slaves—even in church—in case the slaves were planning to rebel.

pants, a jacket, and a shirt made from coarse cloth that scratched his skin. Women wore loose gowns. Children usually ran naked.

The food was not much better. Each week, slaves would get a small portion of cornmeal to bake into cakes, along with salt pork or bacon. Some slaves were allowed to plant vegetables on a small patch of land. Others were able to catch some fish to eat.

For most slaves, hunger was a part of life. "We children had no supper, and only a little piece of bread or something of the kind in the morning," recalled Annie L. Burton, a slave in Alabama.[4]

Richard Toler, a Virginia slave, remembered: "We had very bad eatin'. Bread, meat, water. And they fed it to us in a trough, just like the hogs."[5]

Slaves looked for different ways to fight back. Some pretended to be sick, or they hurt themselves on purpose so they could not work. Others burned down the barns filled with tobacco, rice, and other crops. Some house slaves poisoned their masters by putting deadly plants in their food.[6]

Many slaves joined together to fight for their freedom. The first major slave revolt took place in 1712. Armed with guns,

Some Other Slave Rebellions

1739: The Stono Rebellion: Eighty armed slaves tried to march from Stono, South Carolina, to Florida. They were captured and killed before they had gone fifteen miles.

1800: Blacksmith Gabriel Prosser planned to take over the arsenal in Richmond, Virginia. A storm washed out the roads, and the rebellion never took place

knives, and hatchets, about twenty-five slaves set fire to houses in New York City. Nine white people were killed in the rebellion. The slaves were caught and put to death.[7]

The bloodiest rebellion took place in 1831. A slave named Nat Turner led some followers in a surprise attack on several plantations in Virginia. They killed about sixty white men, women, and children. Like other slave rebellions, Turner's was crushed. As punishment, he was hanged.

A slave's best chance to gain freedom was to run away. No one knows for certain how many slaves escaped. Most historians think that about 100,000 slaves made their way to freedom before the Civil War.[8] Most runaway slaves did not know where they were going. They only knew they were headed North.

CHAPTER 3

★

RUNNING FROM SLAVERY

Escaping slavery was very difficult. The risks were so great that most slaves did not even try.[1] Runaways had to leave their families behind. They might never see their wives, husbands, children, or parents again. If a runaway slave was captured, the punishment was a brutal beating or even death.

The slaves who did try to escape faced constant danger. They suffered hunger and illness. Freezing-cold weather could cause the loss of ears, toes, or fingers. Always there was the fear of being caught. Slave catchers were never far behind with their dogs— usually bloodhounds—who were trained to sniff out runaways.

Young Frederick Douglass, born a slave in Maryland, escaped in 1838.

Some slaves rubbed themselves with onions or the branches of pine trees so the dogs would not be able to pick up their scent.[2]

Running away was so hard that most slaves were only gone for several days. They were usually caught, or they decided on their own to return home.[3]

Yet there were many slaves who were determined to make their way to freedom. "O, that I were free!" said Frederick Douglass, who escaped and later became a famous speaker against slavery.

"I will run away. I will not stand it. . . . I have only one life to lose. I had as well be killed running as die standing."[4]

When a slave ran away, he had no special roads to follow. There were no maps. In their songs, slaves shared secret messages. One song was "Follow the Drinking Gourd." The "drinking gourd" meant the Big Dipper, a group of stars shaped like a cup with a long handle. The Big Dipper points to the North Star. Slaves could use this star to show them the way north to freedom.

For hundreds of miles, escaping slaves made their way across mountains and rivers, through forests and swamps. Some ran with chains on their legs. Others had twelve-pound metal collars around their necks and heads. They ate berries in the woods or waited until dark and stole food from farms.

Most of the slaves trying to escape were men ages sixteen to forty. They usually traveled alone; sometimes they went in small groups. Most ran on foot at night when the darkness would hide them. Many hid on boats or trains traveling north. Henry "Box" Brown escaped by squeezing his two-hundred-pound body into

This 1838 newspaper advertisement offered a reward for capturing Henry May, a runaway slave from Louisville, Kentucky.

"Follow the Drinking Gourd"

When the sun comes back and the first quail calls
Follow the Drinking Gourd.
For the old man is a-waiting for to carry you to freedom
If you follow the Drinking Gourd.

This song contains hidden messages of the route to freedom. The first sentence tells slaves to start their escape as the winter is turning to spring: "When the sun comes back and the first quail calls."

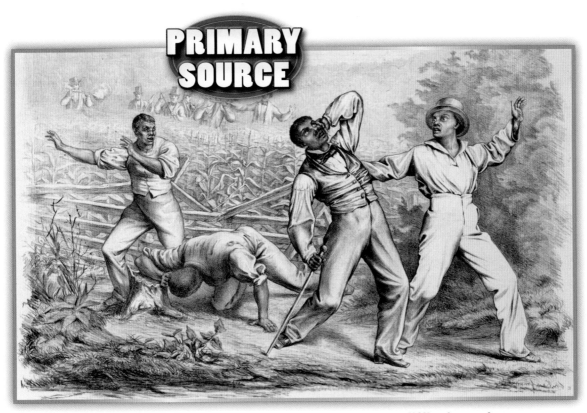

The Fugitive Slave Law made escape even more difficult. It also put more pressure on Northerners to turn in runaway slaves. This political cartoon condemned the law passed by Congress in September 1850.

a small crate in Virginia and having a friend mail him to the free state of Pennsylvania.

When a slave was caught, both the slave and the people who helped him were punished. The Fugitive Slave Law of 1850 made things even worse.[5] Under this law, runaway slaves were no longer safe in the free states of the North. They could still be captured and returned to their masters. Slaves would have to go all the way

William Still was an abolitionist and a conductor on the Underground Railroad.

William Still

William Still, the son of slaves, was in charge of the Underground Railroad in Philadelphia. He kept notes on all the runaway slaves he met. He wrote down their names, where they were from, and more. He hoped his notes would help people find their families.

to Canada before they were truly free. Also, anyone who helped a slave escape could be fined $1,000 or sent to prison for six months.

Still, many people were willing to risk their lives to help runaway slaves. They were part of the Underground Railroad, a secret network of people and escape routes. Some of them had once been slaves. Others just hated slavery.

The Underground Railroad was not underground, and it was not a railroad. According to legend, it got its name around 1831 when a slave named Tice Davids escaped from Kentucky to the free state of Ohio. His owner searched a long time, but never found him. The owner finally gave up, saying the slave must have escaped on "an underground road."[6]

The Underground Railroad was made up of more than 3,200 people—blacks, whites, and American Indians. They offered food, shelter, and money to runaways.

The Underground Railroad was used most from 1830 to 1860. It helped tens of thousands of slaves escape. Some went to the Northern states or to Canada. Others fled south to Mexico and the Caribbean.

CHAPTER 4

★

RIDING THE UNDERGROUND RAILROAD

Because secrecy was very important on the Underground Railroad, it had its own secret language. Runaway slaves were called passengers, packages, or freight. The people leading slaves to freedom were conductors. Slaves were hidden in homes called stations, which were run by stationmasters. Anyone providing money or goods to help the railroad was called a stockholder.

The conductors often used their own homes as stations. These stations were ten to twenty miles apart. The slaves were hidden in secret rooms in the attic or cellar. Sometimes hiding spaces were built inside fake cupboards. Other homes had bookcases that hid

UNCLE
TOM'S CABIN.
BY
HARRIET BEECHER STOWE.
WITH
Twenty-seven Illustrations on Wood
BY
GEORGE CRUIKSHANK, ESQ.

EVA AND TOPSY.

LONDON:
JOHN CASSELL, LUDGATE HILL.
1852.

The title page to an 1852 edition of Harriet Beecher Stowe's novel *Uncle Tom's Cabin*.

Abolitionist Weapons

The Underground Railroad was not the only weapon that abolitionists used against slavery.

★ In 1831, William Lloyd Garrison began publishing an anti-slavery newspaper called *The Liberator*.

★ In 1851, Harriet Beecher Stowe wrote a book called *Uncle Tom's Cabin*. The story described slaves as real people. This book did more than anything else to turn Northerners against slavery.

the stairs to the cellar. Outside, haystacks were used to cover up tunnels that took runaways to secret places. Barns often had false floors with some space below for a person to hide.

Harriet Jacobs, a runaway slave, squeezed herself into the tiny crawl space of an attic with mice, rats, and insects. "I lived in that little dismal hole, almost deprived of light and air, and with no space to move my limbs, for nearly seven years," she said. "Yet I would have chosen this, rather than my lot as a slave."[1] She finally escaped to freedom with the help of the Underground Railroad.

Conductors helped guide slaves from station to station as they made their way north. It was very hard for a slave to lose himself in a crowd during the day.[2] His skin color made him stand out among white people. In the daytime, a runaway might hide in a barn, a cave, or a wagon filled with hay. Then he would travel to the next station in the dark of night.

Different signals let runaways know which houses were part of the Underground Railroad. Often, lighted candles or lanterns were used to mark stations. White bricks at the top of a chimney also meant a house was safe. When a slave arrived at a station,

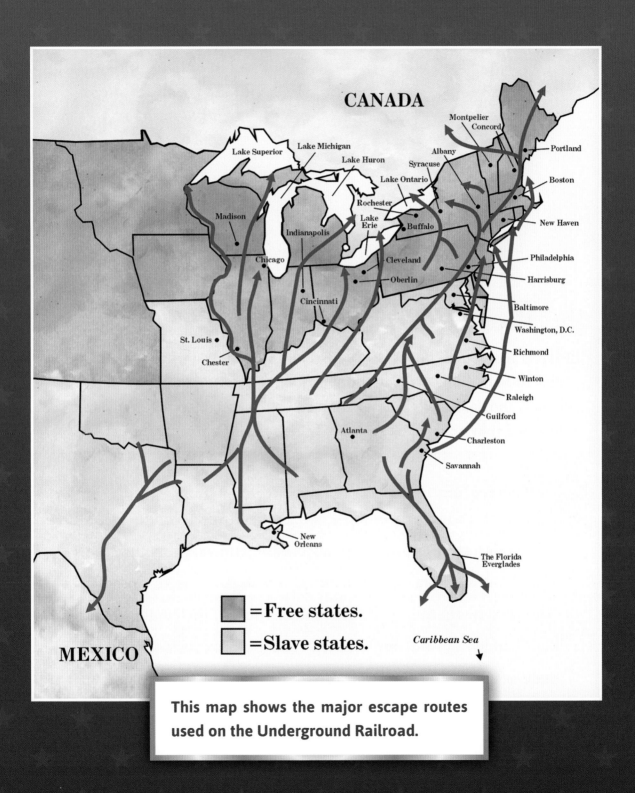

This map shows the major escape routes used on the Underground Railroad.

Despite the help of brave conductors and stationmasters, as well as the many stations along the Underground Railroad routes, slaves still faced a difficult and dangerous journey to freedom. Escape often required daring plans and risky actions to reach safety in the Northern states or Canada.

he could identify himself by giving a special knock, hooting like an owl, or using a password he had learned from a conductor.

The greatest number of successful runaways came from Maryland, Virginia, and Kentucky.[3] These states were closest to the free states in the North. One major route of the Underground Railroad led slaves from Kentucky and Virginia through the free state of Ohio. Another well-traveled route ran from Maryland across Pennsylvania into New England or Canada.

Slaves in North Carolina, South Carolina, Georgia, Alabama, Mississippi, and Florida had to travel six hundred to seven hundred miles before reaching a free state. They were less likely to succeed. To escape from the Deep South, many runaways needed to sneak onto a boat sailing north on the Atlantic Ocean.

Mary Millburn fled from Norfolk, Virginia, in 1858. Workers on the Underground Railroad arranged for her to travel on a steamship to Philadelphia. When Mary was told to dress in men's clothing, she said, "Any way so I succeed."[4] After arriving safely in Philadelphia, Mary continued on to Boston.

True Believers

Like many other abolitionists, Thomas Garrett was a Quaker. Quakers believed all people were equal. They had been working to get rid of slavery since the American Revolution. By the 1840s, there were more than two thousand antislavery societies in the North. Most of the 250,000 members were Quakers. They gave lectures and wrote newspaper and magazine articles calling for an end to slavery.

After escaping slavery herself, Harriet Tubman became a legendary conductor on the Underground Railroad.

James Mercer, William H. Gilliam, and John Clayton escaped from their owners in Richmond, Virginia, and also stowed away on a steamship. The only place they could hide was near the ship's boiler, which was so hot that the steward who helped them was not sure if they would survive. The men had to lie flat on the floor with no light and little air.

Yet the three slaves were determined to escape. When their ship docked in the North, the men traveled to a station along the Underground Railroad. They were soaked from a heavy rainstorm . . . but they were free.

John Henry Hill broke away from a slave auction in Virginia just as he was about to be handcuffed. Kicking and fighting with his hands and feet, Hill ran and hid. "Nine months I was trying to get away," he said.[5] Hill hid in the kitchen of a safe house. Then he traveled by steamboat to Philadelphia.

Harriet Tubman, a slave in Maryland, followed the North Star and escaped to Philadelphia. She went on to become the most famous conductor on the Underground Railroad. Tubman risked her life nineteen times, returning to the South to help other slaves escape to freedom.

"I had reasoned this out in my mind," Tubman said about her escape. "There was one of two things I had a right to, liberty or death; if I could not have one, I would have the other."[6]

CHAPTER 5

WORKING ON THE RAILROAD

Many different people worked for the Underground Railroad. Yet they all had one thing in common: They believed it was wrong for one man to own another. They wanted to help abolish slavery.

Levi Coffin was one of the best-known stationmasters on the railroad. He always kept a team of horses and a wagon ready to aid runaway slaves. "These journeys had to be made at night, often through deep mud and bad roads," he wrote. "Slave hunters were often on the track, and sometimes ahead of the slaves."[1]

Over the years, Coffin shared his home with more than 3,000 slaves as they made their way to freedom.

Harriet Tubman led more than three hundred slaves out of the South and said she "never lost a single passenger."[2] She carried a gun for protection on her dangerous journeys with runaway slaves. Tubman was also ready to shoot anyone who became scared and wanted to turn back. That would put the lives of the others at risk. "You go on or die!" she would say, pointing her gun at their heads.[3] By 1856, there was a $40,000 reward offered for her capture.

Another worker on the railroad with a price on his head was Thomas Garrett. He offered his Wilmington, Delaware, house as a station for slaves escaping to the free state of Pennsylvania. Garrett helped nearly three thousand slaves. A reward of $10,000 was advertised for his arrest.[4]

Many times, slaveholders with guns and knives would arrive at Garrett's house. They demanded to know where their slaves were hiding. But Garrett never told them anything. He would push away their weapons, saying that only cowards needed to use guns and knives.[5]

Sojourner Truth

Sojourner Truth was born into slavery in 1797. Many years later, free at last, she began traveling around the country giving speeches against slavery. She was one of the most famous abolitionists of the time.

Sojourner Truth

Jane Cannon was born in Pennsylvania. She began working for the Underground Railroad after moving to Kentucky. Cannon ran her own antislavery newspaper.[6] When her printing press was destroyed by an angry mob, Cannon simply bought another one. She would not stop publishing articles against slavery.[7]

The father of Kentucky slave William Wells Brown was a white plantation owner. But Brown's mother was a slave, so he was a slave. When he was twenty, Brown escaped to freedom and became a conductor on the Underground Railroad. Working on board a steamboat on Lake Erie, he took runaways to Canada.

Frederick Douglass was a very important abolitionist. Born a slave in Maryland, he escaped to Massachusetts at the age of twenty-one. Douglass taught himself to read and write. He became famous for speaking out against slavery, and he worked very hard to help the Underground Railroad.

The Price They Paid

Many people who worked on the Underground Railroad were caught and punished.

★ Jonathan Walker, a sea captain, was found smuggling slaves from Florida to the Bahamas. The slaves were returned to their owner and Walker had "SS"—for "Slave Stealer"—branded on his right hand. He also spent eight months in jail.

★ Calvin Fairbanks spent sixteen years in a Kentucky prison for helping slaves escape to Canada.

★ Charles Turner Torrey aided more than 400 slaves on their way to freedom. He was caught and thrown into a Baltimore prison.[8]

When Abraham Lincoln was elected president in November 1860, many Southerners feared that he would end slavery. In December 1860, a month after Lincoln's victory, South Carolina seceded from the Union. More Southern states followed, forming the Confederacy.

"As a means of destroying slavery, it [the Underground Railroad] was like an attempt to bail out the ocean with a teaspoon," Douglass wrote, "but the thought that there was *one* less slave, brought to my heart unspeakable joy."[9]

For years, Southerners had watched antislavery feelings spread across much of the United States. When Abraham Lincoln was

The Proclamation

The Emancipation Proclamation, by President Lincoln, freed all slaves in the rebelling Confederate States of America. But the Confederacy had its own president and did not obey Lincoln. So the proclamation did not really free any slaves. Still, it was important because it showed the world that the Civil War was now a fight to end slavery.

elected president in 1860, they worried that he would put an end to slavery throughout the country. Without slaves, they would lose most of their workers . . . and a lot of money.

The Southern states decided to take action. In December 1860, South Carolina was the first to secede—or break away—from the United States. Soon, ten more Southern states followed. They called themselves the Confederate States of America. They said they were no longer part of the United States.

When the Civil War broke out in April 1861, Lincoln said he was fighting to keep the nation together. He did not want the

By the President of the United States of America:

A Proclamation.

Whereas, on the twenty-second day of September, in the year of our Lord one thousand eight hundred and sixty-two, a proclamation was issued by the President of the United States, containing, among other things, the following, to wit:

"That on the first day of January, in the year of our Lord one thousand eight hundred and sixty-three, all persons held as slaves within any State or designated part of a State, the people whereof shall then be in rebellion against the United States, shall be then, thenceforward, and forever free; and the Executive Government of the United States, including the military and naval authority thereof, will recognize and maintain the freedom of such persons, and will do no act or acts to repress such persons, or any of them, in any efforts they may make for their actual freedom.

"That the Executive will, on the first day

This is page one of the Emancipation Proclamation. President Lincoln issued this law on January 1, 1863, granting freedom to all slaves in the rebelling Southern states. Although this document did not free all slaves, it was a necessary first step in eliminating the evil institution from the United States forever.

Freedom and the Law

★ In 1865, the Thirteenth Amendment to the Constitution abolished slavery throughout the United States.

★ In 1868, the Fourteenth Amendment gave black citizens equal protection under the law and the right to hold a political office.

★ Two years later, the Fifteenth Amendment gave black men the right to vote.

United States split into two countries. Yet slavery had always been at the root of the bad feelings between the North and South.

In 1863, Lincoln issued the Emancipation Proclamation. This document freed the slaves in the rebelling Southern states. The war had openly become a fight over slavery.

The Civil War lasted four years, taking the lives of more than 600,000 men. In April 1865, the South finally surrendered to the North. The country was united again.

Four million slaves were now free. They needed jobs, and they needed education. They would struggle to be treated fairly. But after nearly 250 years, black Americans were no longer in chains.

It was a beginning.

TIMELINE

1600s

1619: African slaves are sold in Jamestown, Virginia.

1642: Slavery becomes legal in the Massachusetts Bay Colony.

1662: Virginia law states that slaves from Africa will remain slaves for life.

1700s

1777: Slavery is abolished in Vermont.

1780: Slavery is abolished in Massachusetts and Pennsylvania.

1784: Laws are set up to begin abolishing slavery in Connecticut and Rhode Island.

1793: The first Fugitive Slave Act makes it against the law to help runaway slaves.

- The cotton gin is invented, giving new life to the slave industry in the South.

1799: New York begins to abolish slavery.

1800s

1800: Free blacks in Philadelphia ask the U.S. Congress to abolish slavery (their request was voted down 85 to 1).

Early 1800s: The Underground Railroad is first organized.

1803: Cotton becomes the leading export crop of the United States.

1804: New Jersey begins to abolish slavery.

1808: Importing slaves is outlawed.

1818: Ten states allow slavery, and ten states do not.

Timeline

1831: The Underground Railroad begins its busiest period of activity, which will last for 30 years.

- William Lloyd Garrison begins publishing *The Liberator*.

1845: Texas becomes a state, and slavery is permitted there.

1849: California outlaws slavery.

1850: The second Fugitive Slave Law is passed.

1859: John Brown attacks the U.S. arsenal at Harper's Ferry, Virginia.

1860: Abraham Lincoln is elected president of the United States.

- South Carolina secedes from the United States.

1861: Six more Southern states secede, and the Confederate States of America is formed, with Jefferson Davis as president.

- **April:** Shots are fired at Fort Sumter, and the Civil War begins.
- Four more Southern states secede.

1863: Lincoln issues the Emancipation Proclamation.

- **July:** The Union wins the Battle of Gettysburg.
- **November:** President Lincoln gives the Gettysburg Address.

1864: Ulysses S. Grant is named commander of the Union army.

- **November:** Lincoln is elected to a second term as president.

1865: Confederate general Robert E. Lee surrenders to Union general Ulysses S. Grant.

- **April:** President Lincoln is assassinated. Andrew Johnson becomes president.
- **December:** The Thirteenth Amendment to the U.S. Constitution abolishes slavery in the United States.

CHAPTER NOTES

CHAPTER 1. THE GROWTH OF SLAVERY

1. Milton Meltzer, *Slavery: A World History* (New York: Da Capo Press, 1993), vol. 2, p. 51.
2. Lerone Bennett, Jr., *The Shaping of Black America* (Chicago: Johnson Publishing Company, Inc., 1975), p. 8.
3. Peter Kolchin, *American Slavery: 1619–1877* (New York: Hill & Wang, 1993), pp. 12–13.
4. "List and Inventory of Negroes on Plantation . . . ," *Africans in America*, n.d., <http://www.pbs.org/wgbh/aia/part3/3h503.html> (June 3, 2003).
5. Charles Johnson, Patricia Smith, and the WGBH Series Research Team, *Africans in America: America's Journey Through Slavery* (New York: Harcourt, Brace & Company, 1998), p. 41.
6. Ibid., p. 111.
7. *A Century of Population Growth: From the First Census of the United States to the Twelfth,* 1790–1900 (Baltimore, Md.: Genealogical Publishing Co., 1970), p. 80.

CHAPTER 2. THE LIFE OF A SLAVE

1. Lerone Bennett, Jr., *Before the Mayflower: A History of Black America* (Chicago: Johnson Publishing Company, Inc., 1969), p. 95.
2. William Wells Brown, *Narrative of William Wells Brown, An American Slave* (London: Charles Gilpin, 1849), p. 15.
3. Charles Johnson and Patricia Smith, *Africans in America: America's Journey Through Slavery* (New York: Harcourt Brace & Company, 1998), p. 87.
4. Annie L. Burton, *Memories of Childhood's Slavery Days* (Boston: Ross Publishing Company, 1909), p. 4.
5. George P. Rawick, ed., *The American Slave: A Composite Autobiography* (Westport, Conn.: Greenwood Press, 1972–9), vol. 16, p. 100. This is a transcription of testimonies of ex-slaves, collected by employees of the Federal Writers' Project of the Work Project Administration (WPA) in the 1930s. Each narrative tells one slave's story, but read together, they give a composite view of slavery.
6. William R. Scott and William G. Shade, *Upon These Shores: Themes in the African-American Experience 1600 to the Present* (New York: Routledge, 2000), p. 94.
7. Alton Hornsby, Jr., *Chronology of African-American History* (Detroit, Mich.: Gale Research, 1997), p. 4.
8. Underground Railroad, *Official National Park Handbook,* Division of Publications, National Parks Service, U.S. Department of the Interior, Washington, D.C., 1998, p. 54.

CHAPTER 3. RUNNING FROM SLAVERY

1. Underground Railroad, *Official National Park Handbook,* Division of Publications, National Parks Service, U.S. Department of the Interior, Washington, D.C., 1998, p. 52.
2. Charles Johnson and Patricia Smith, *Africans in America: America's Journey Through Slavery* (New York: Harcourt Brace & Company, 1998), p. 366.
3. Kenneth M. Stampp, *The Peculiar Institution: Slavery in the Ante-Bellum South* (New York: Alfred A. Knopf, 1967), p. 115.

4. John W. Blassingame, *The Slave Community: Plantation Life in the Ante-Bellum South* (New York: Oxford University Press, 1972), p. 104.
5. Peter Kolchin, *American Slavery: 1619–1877* (New York: Hill and Wang, 1993), p. 84.
6. Wilbur H. Siebert, *The Underground Railroad from Slavery to Freedom* (New York: Macmillan Company, 1898), p. 33.

CHAPTER 4. RIDING THE UNDERGROUND RAILROAD

1. "Judgement Day: Fugitive Slaves and Northern Racism," *Africans in America,* n.d., <www.pbs.org/wgbh/aia/part4/4narr3.html> (June 3, 2003).
2. William J. Cooper, Jr. and Thomas E. Terrill, *The American South: A History* (New York: Alfred A. Knopf, 1990), p. 239.
3. Kenneth M. Stampp, *The Peculiar Institution: Slavery in the Ante-Bellum South* (New York: Alfred A. Knopf, 1967), p. 118.
4. William Still, *The Underground Railroad: A Record* (Chicago: Johnson Publishing Company Inc., 1970), p. 584.
5. Ibid., p. 191.
6. "The Underground Railroad," *History Channel,* n.d., <www.historychannel.com/exhibits/undergroundrr/story.html> (June 3, 2003).

CHAPTER 5. WORKING ON THE RAILROAD

1. "Levi Coffin's Underground Railroad Station," *Africans in America,* n.d., <www.pbs.org/wgbh/aia/part4/4h2946t.html> (June 3, 2003).
2. "Fugitive Slaves and Northern Racism—People and Events: Harriet Tubman," *Africans in America,* n.d., <www.pbs.org/wgbh/aia/part4/4p1535.html> (June 3, 2003).
3. James Simkin, "The Slave Trade: Underground Railroad," *Spartacus Educational,* May 2, 2003, <www.spartacus.schoolnet.co.uk/USASunderground.htm> (June 3, 2003).
4. Robert C. Smedley, *History of the Underground Railroad in Chester and the Neighboring Counties of Pennsylvania* (New York: Negro Universities Press, 1968), p. 238.
5. William Still, *The Underground Railroad: A Record* (Chicago: Johnson Publishing Company Inc., 1970), p. 649.
6. Jane Cannon Swisshelm, "What's in the News," Pennsylvania State University, Penn State Public Broadcasting, <http://www.witn.psu.edu/activities/newsmaker.phtml?show_id=10> (June 3, 2003).
7. Frederick Douglass, *The Life and Times of Frederick Douglass* (Hartford, Conn.: Park Publishing Co., 1881), p. 266.
8. Underground Railroad, *Official National Park Handbook,* Division of Publications, National Parks Service, U.S. Department of the Interior, Washington, D.C., 1998, p. 63.
9. Douglass, p. 272.

GLOSSARY

abolitionist—Person who wants to put an end to slavery.

amendment—A change made to the U.S. Constitution.

cotton gin—A machine that separates the cotton seeds from the cotton fiber. The word gin stands for engine.

emancipation—Setting someone free.

gourd—A fruit that grows on a vine, like a pumpkin. Gourds are not for eating. They can be dried and then carved into bowls, cups, and dippers.

indentured servant—A person who must work for no pay for several years before being given his or her freedom.

Quaker—A Christian religious group that opposes war and believes in the equality of men and women.

rebellion—An armed uprising.

slave—A person who is the property of someone else and can be bought and sold.

FURTHER READING

★

Books

Allen, Thomas B. *Harriet Tubman, Secret Agent: How Daring Slaves and Free Blacks Spied for the Union During the Civil War.* Washington, D.C.: National Geographic, 2009.

Fradin, Dennis Brindell. *The Underground Railroad.* New York: Marshall Cavendish Benchmark, 2012.

Landau, Elaine. *Fleeing to Freedom on the Underground Railroad: The Courageous Slaves, Agents, and Conductors.* Minneapolis, Minn.: Twenty-First Century Books, 2006.

Osborne, Linda Barrett. *Traveling the Freedom Road: From Slavery and the Civil War Through Reconstruction.* New York: Abrams Books for Young Readers, 2009.

Internet Addresses

National Geographic Education: The Underground Railroad
<http://education.nationalgeographic.com/education/multimedia/interactive/the-underground-railroad/?ar_a=1>

The Underground Railroad: Escape From Slavery Student Activity
<http://teacher.scholastic.com/activities/bhistory/underground_railroad/index.htm>

INDEX